ASHLYN'S JOURNAL

A FATHER'S EXPERIENCE FOLLOWING
HIS BABY DAUGHTER'S DEATH

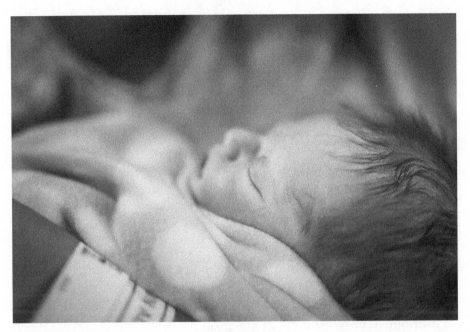

Ashlyn Marie
June 20, 2016
6 lbs. 12.8 oz.
19.5 in.

ANDREW YACKUBOSKEY

ISBN 978-1-64258-050-1 (paperback)
ISBN 978-1-64258-130-0 (hardcover)
ISBN 978-1-64258-051-8 (digital)

Christian Faith Publishing, Inc.
832 Park Avenue
Meadville, PA 16335
www.christianfaithpublishing.com

Printed in the United States of America

For Ashlyn,

These words are not meant to cheapen your
life or death. If they do, I'm so sorry.

Love forever and always,
Your Daddy

P.S. Love isn't a strong enough word to describe the feeling I have for
you.

PREFACE

The following journal is one dad's account of his feelings and emotions in the year following his daughter's death. This is in no way, shape, or form a substitute for forming your own thoughts and feelings about your own life.

~*~

A lot of what is written here was unedited because I wanted to preserve the rawness of it, the realness of what we went through. I feel it was much more important than any grammar errors that you might find.

On June 20, 2016, our lives would forever be changed. I remember the day like it was yesterday. I worked the midnight shift and all was normal until I got home around 9:30 a.m. My wife was completely distraught as she told me she couldn't feel our baby move at all. I tried my best to remain calm but inside I feared the worst. We tried everything, from feeding my wife leftover Father's Day cake to induce a sugar high to get Ashlyn to move. I tried talking into her belly to get her to respond or wake up.

In every effort, every attempt, there was nothing. Nothing but stillness. We called the doctors and they told us to meet them at the hospital. Driving there was the longest drive of my life, a half hour drive felt more like a twenty-four-hour drive. On the outside I was calm, collected, and completely relaxed. On the inside, I was in a full out panic and extremely stressed out.

~*~

It was the hummingbirds that restored our hope and faith. The messengers sent from above, they were everywhere.

~*~

When my wife looked up at me with such pain and agony, there's no words in this language can describe.

~*~

You can cry your rest of your life
But
Know that Ashlyn is happy
And she wants
Us to be happy too.

~*~

I must live a good life so I can be reunited with her.

June 20–June 30

Reflection: On Living a Simpler Life

You must live a much simpler life. A life worth living. A life using all of God's gifts and talents he gave you.

The Parable of the Talents (Matt. 25:14–30)

It will be as when a man who was going on a journey called in his servants and entrusted his possessions to them. To one he gave five talents; to another, two; to a third, one—to each according to his ability. Then he went away. Immediately the one who received five talents went and traded with them, and made another five. Likewise, the one who received two made another two. But the man who received one went off and dug a hole in the ground and buried his master's money. After a long time, the master of those servants came back and settled accounts with them. The one who had received five talents came forward bringing the additional five. He said, 'Master, you gave me five talents. See, I have made five more.' His master said to him, 'Well done, my good and faithful servant. Since you were faithful in small matters, I will give you great responsibilities. Come, share your master's joy.' [Then] the one who had received two talents also came forward and said, 'Master, you gave me two talents. See, I have made two more.' His master said to him, 'Well done, my good and faithful servant. Since you were faithful in small matters, I will give you great responsibilities. Come, share your master's joy.' Then the one who had received the one talent came forward and said, 'Master, I knew you were a demanding person, harvesting where you did not plant and gathering where you did not scatter; so out of fear I went off and buried your talent in the ground. Here it is back.' His master said to him in reply, 'You wicked, lazy servant! So you knew that I harvest where I did not plant and gather where I did not scatter? Should you not then have put my money in the bank with interest on my return? Now then! Take the talent from him and give it to the one with ten. For to everyone who has, more will be given and he will grow rich; but from the one who has not, even what he has will be taken away. And throw this useless servant into the darkness outside, where there will be wailing and grinding of teeth.'

Room 5908

Why was I freezing to death in a climate-controlled room for two days? I kept checking the room's thermostat and it read seventy degrees every time, even seventy-one degrees at one point when more people were in the room, so how was it I was shivering so? Was it because I was going into some form of shock? Maybe, but that doesn't seem to explain the long span of time I was freezing wearing layers of clothes, shivering.

I thought maybe it's the vent in the ceiling, it's loud it seems to be blowing air. I put my hand up to the vent and nothing. No cool air just background noise from the duct workings.

There has been too much I've experienced in life, too many unexplainable incidents to deny the inevitable fact that we are NOT alone. I find comfort in the fact that my baby daughter was there with me, watching her family, her mom and dad, watching us mourn her passing because we loved her so, so much. I hope she felt our love, because we felt hers and I will never forget that feeling. That gentle sweetness I could feel from my baby girl.

On Going Back to Work

I'll kill someone if I go back.
I won't be able to hold my tongue or my fist.
Not after what I've been through.
Obviously, I'm not going to let my family starve... or lose the roof over our heads. But after this horrible tragedy, it's really opened my eyes, life is short and I can do anything. There's nothing to fear.
Not after what we've gone through. I laugh in the face of death. I've been to worst places now.

$-*-$

There are no breaks (for us) only suffering.

When I forget the "feeling" of her, that'll be another deathblow to me. It will be like losing her all over again. I hope that day does not come soon.

When the routine of life reaches me that will be another gut shot as well. It will be like closing one chapter in my life that I desperately want to keep open in the hopes that she'll return like this has been just a horrible nightmare, I'll wake up one day and starting a whole new chapter without her and realizing she's gone because she's not in it (and she's never coming back) that'll be like losing her all over again too.

Monday

At 5:46 p.m. Ashlyn stillborn at the hospital.

She was 6 lbs. 12.8 oz., 19 ½ inches long. Head full of hair just like her brothers.

Tuesday

2:00 p.m., meeting with funeral home.

Wednesday

9:30 a.m., meeting with Queen of Heaven Cemetery.
10:00 a.m.–2:00 p.m., drop off Ashlyn's burial outfit.
Evening, told Gavin, Ashlyn passed away.

Thursday

9:00 a.m.–10:00 a.m., viewing.
10:00 a.m., funeral service at the funeral home with Father Freeny.
11:00 a.m., Queen of Heaven Cemetery carried casket to gravesite.
Afternoon luncheon at parents' home.

Keepsakes for Ashlyn

Here is a collection of items we laid to rest with our precious daughter, Ashlyn.

Her pink cross from above her bedroom door.

Two pink binkies.

White dress.

Three picture frames (mommy kissing Ashlyn, daddy kissing Ashlyn, all three of us together).

White blanket.

Bear (from big brother Ryan).

Original letter (from Daddy).

Pearl bracelet (from Mommy).

~*~

My wedding ring, my cross necklace, and my wristband were all pressed against her sweet lips.

~*~

We came to the hospital three days before our daughter passed away and these are the questions we walked away with after Dr. X never even came in to check on my wife and daughter.

ANGER

Dr. X,

Did you know she had a miscarriage at twelve weeks?

Did you know her son was born at thirty-four weeks?

Did you know she was getting progesterone shots every week?

Did you know she had protein in her urine?

Did you know she was 4 cm dilated and 90 percent effaced?

Did you know she was high risk?

Did you know she was sent to a specialist, Dr. T? Did you know he was trying to do everything he could to get her to thirty-seven weeks?

Did you know she was thirty-eight weeks and four days?

Did you know she was hospitalized at twenty-nine weeks with this pregnancy?

Did you know she was in constant pain and contractions? Which is it Dr. X? Neglect or Malpractice? OR BOTH?

Restoring Faith in Humanity

Do you know what it's like to have a complete and total stranger cry and pour their hearts out for you?

It's incredible.

It restores my faith in humanity… a little bit.

It's hard to see the pain or even harder to see the "no pain" as people try to scramble for the words to speak in a situation where no words are necessary or applicable.

We are all called. We are all God's children.

Many will be called; few will be chosen.

You were one of the chosen ones.

My
    Dear
        Sweet
            Baby
                Angel.

The Day After the Funeral

We ate. We printed more pictures of her. We cried. We played with Ryan, the shining light of the world everyone crowds around to get warm.

I did some of the stupid routines in life. Paid bills, mowed grass, etc.

~*~

Pretty dark. Pretty depressing.
The nothing.

~*~

One in a thousand they tell us. One in a thousand like it's supposed to make you feel better. You never think that one is going to be you. It's always someone else. Until it happens. You're the one. Ninety-nine point nine percent of the time, you're good! Well, not us. We were the one.

June 20, 2016

9:50 a.m., we call the doctor's office, we're told go to the hospital.
10:50 a.m., we arrive at the hospital.

Thirty-seventh week apt they messed up the time and said they were too busy and come back next week, but they'd see her if she had the "appointment card."

Thirty-eight weeks and four days. Dr. X didn't even check on her at the hospital.

Thirty-nine weeks. My baby girl passes away.

Dr. X says, "See you in six weeks."

Friday, June 25, no call yet. Got a sympathy card June 28, 2016. Most impersonal card ever. I'll get the best lawyer in the world and stick 'em to a wall.

One in a thousand. They tell us. Just a case of bad luck, they say.

Extremely angry and extremely sad and feel nothing at the same time.

Tuesday Night, June 21, 2016

Tuesday, told Gavin his baby sister passed away. I drove around until I found a park, Gavin fell asleep in the backseat by the time I found the place. We got out and played catch with a baseball. Gavin was noticeably irritated and started crying for no reason, he probably suspects something isn't right. I walk over to him and pull him in close hugging him and tell him his sister passed away and he collapses into my arms and asks why. I have no response. I just cry with him and hold him tight.

I show him her (your) picture later that night and he starts crying, he says Ashlyn (you) look just like Ryan.

On Trust

There was trust Thursday (June 16, 2016). The trust in the doctors is GONE now. I felt the same way today as I did then. They should've induced her, but hey, what do I know? I'm just a dumb coal miner.

I feel like I could breathe fire and vomit at the same time.

I feel like someone is choking me. It's like getting slammed in the chest with a sledgehammer every fifteen minutes. It's like dying over and over again.

You try to make sense of things and you can't. I don't know why things happen for a reason or why things are but what I do know is… I had a daughter whom I loved very much, she's gone now, my heart is broken but that doesn't change the love I have for her. You have to keep the faith and a priest told me, God needs little angels.

Ashlyn was born at 5:46 p.m. on June 20, 2016, MONDAY.

On Family and Support

Thank you all for your love and support. In our very desperate time of need, we are all in this together and we'll make it through. We have to. Because that's what Ashlyn would've wanted.

Cloud of baby with wings in the sky on a walk.

We have to keep our eyes open to the signs all the time.
Live life to the fullest.
It's far too short.
Don't wait for a tragedy to happen.

_*_

You are the most beautiful baby I have ever seen.
I won't make it because I'm strong, I'll make it because God will carry me. He has to.
I feel like the whole world knows and pities me.
Everyone has been so kind, even those who don't know. Maybe it's the sorrow in my eyes.
Ninety-six point ninety-six times. That's how many times I die every day, about every fifteen minutes, with little to no sleep, about one hundred times a day.

_*_

3:00 a.m. writing, it's late or early depending on which way you look at it or I guess it depends on the time you went to sleep.
Hey, you can bother me any time you want Ashlyn.
But I know you're in a better place and that comforts me. I won't be strong with you not here, God will have to carry me, so let God know that since your up there.
And until we meet again...
Love forever and always, your daddy.
Yesterday was the worst day of my life... until today. Having to bury your own child is something no parent should have to endure.
I will lead a good life to get into heaven so I can be reunited with my baby girl.
If she's not there, I'll find a way to get to her. We will be reunited one way or another that's for sure. I'll kick St. Peter in the shin or something at the gates (at Heaven's gate) if I have to.
How much value is one's life worth?

I can't go back to work. I can't go back doing the same thing as before like nothing ever happened. I cannot and will not.

I blame that black hole in the ground.

I'm not afraid to die anymore. I love being mortal. It means I get to see her one day again.

I'll either be reunited with my baby daughter or my pain will be eased. Either way I win.

The feeling of not being afraid to die anymore is very "uplifting."

June 24, 2016

Every day is a bad day because your (Ashlyn) not here.

But I guess every day, is a day closer till we meet again.

There are no "good" days. Not anymore.

I believe writers are at least internally naturally dark people, because happy people enjoy being just that happy. Happy and doing nothing else.

~*~

Every day is just a blur. I can't remember what day it is, ever since that dark day. Does it really matter what day it is? It's just the earth spinning and man calling it whatever day he wants to. Why can't Thursday be Tuesday? And so on and so forth? Who cares?

There really is no "I'm fine" anymore. "I'm fine" is just translation for "I don't intend on killing myself today." There is no "I'm fine" anymore. Not for us. How can we be? Our baby girl is gone.

A simple question like "how are you?" has a new twist now. "How are you?" What does that even mean? How am I? How am I compared to the average person? How am I compared to how I normally feel? How am I compared to a terminally ill cancer patient? I mean, what does "how are you" even mean? Does it mean how am I compared to my usual self? Or how I think I should be? You don't know my usual self so what does my answer even mean to you? How am I? How am I supposed to be? Even the smallest questions become confusing and exhausting.

~*~

I'm not sure who this new person is. I'd like to think that I'm better. That I'm stronger. But I'm hurt. Destroyed and shattered. So, I'm not sure who this new person staring back at me in the mirror truly is. He's angry. He's hurt. He's in pain. He's suffering. I can see all of these things. There is no happiness anymore in this man, no state of being happy. Only moments with less pain.

Why do we cry? Why do we laugh? Physiological responses to emotions. Why?

I better get a doctor and get checked up and make sure I'm not dying because I feel like I'm rotting away from the inside out.

~*~

What do you do when you can't give your wife the one thing she wants?

You (Ashlyn).

ALL MOM WANTS IS YOU.

She cried tears of joy when she found out you were here at the gender reveal ultrasound.

She cried tears of sorrow when she found out you were gone.

WHY GOD WHY? AFTER THIS YOU HAVE TO CARRY ME! YOU HAVE TO! *I scream through a shower of tears.*

~*~

June 25, 2016

I'm writing about you, you must be here. I'm happy to "see" you. Happy to "feel" you. Happy you're here (in spirit).

~*~

July

I still drive the same stretch of highway. Still stare at the same sun. It's like nothing has changed, like nothing cares. Like she never existed and that hurts. It hurts a deep searing pain inside like being cut in half by a hot sword.

But **everything** is different now. Sad and depressing with you not here anymore and knowing you're never going to be here. It hurts. It hurts so freakin' bad.

I have a lot to figure out in the month of July and my heart is in pieces… if it's even still there at all.

It is only after we are not afraid to be mortal, we become invincible… and can do anything.

The irony is we don't care if we die and that makes you as close to immortal as you can get on earth.

~*~

My wife's heart. Her heart. Our hearts were completely shattered. Destroyed. I wouldn't have been surprised if my wife passed away because her heart had stopped (quit working).

~*~

Every Night is restless sleep.
Every Morning the cold reality slams you hard in the chest.
She was my baby girl and Ryan's Irish Twin.
My head feels too heavy to wear a hat.

No matter how much sleep I get I feel like a train hit me when I wake up. They say that it's due to emotional trauma. I guess that must be true.

Reasons Not to Drink

The promise.
Can't stop.
Don't want to forget the feeling of what she felt like in my arms.

~*~

So, I made a list of things I still care about.
Family.
That's it. The single most important thing glaring at me, pleading with me, shouting at me.
Family.
FAMILY.
FAMILY!
Sure, you can add God and friends to that short list, but I already consider both an important integral part of "family."
Notice the list doesn't include food, a thousand channels, sports, weather, cars, a mansion or any other bullshit possession you can think of.
Live a much simpler life. That's what God wants you to do. He knows that doing only that will make you truly happy.
And family members sometimes have more than two feet.

~*~

On Condolences

You can never have enough prayers and we need as many as people are willing to give.

‑*‑

I just don't want to stop thinking about that day. About her. About the way she felt in my arms. I don't want to let go, to lose that "feeling." When I do, it will be a very, very dark day. The day when I can no longer remember what she "feels" like.

I often think about that day. The day in the future I forget what she felt like. Thinking about that looming day makes me break down and cry.

‑*‑

Stillbirths

Your own child passing is not something you prepare for. How can you? The mere one-second thought causes too much pain to bear, when it became a reality. It was a total nightmare, in the worse sense of things. I wish I could trade places with you (Ashlyn) in an instant. But then how selfish can I be? How could I take you away from a place so beautiful, so happy, so filling with joy? And bring you into a world filled with so much darkness and despair. A world without your daddy because I traded places with you. You stay where you are, honey, my sweet angel, I'll lead a good life in your name and honor, and when God is ready we will be reunited again.

God, it hurts so much.

Her body is just that. It's her body, her earthly vessel to navigate this world. And when she's gone that's not her anymore. Her spirit is gone from here (Earth) and off to a place we can't imagine.

I'm not sure how long the spirit sticks around the body after the lungs stop breathing or the heart stops beating, but your own spirit can sense other spirits around other life. I can tell you it felt so comforting and so crushing to hold my baby in my arms. You (Ashlyn) were there. Either floating around me or inside your body your earthly vessel still. I can tell you I froze to death for two days in a seventy-degree temperature climate-controlled room. She was there.

They say angels are messengers and that God needs little angels. It's hard to comprehend. Extremely hard to understand, but Ashlyn has taught me so much, more than anyone in my lifetime put together. And the message is loud and clear.

This world means everything and nothing at once. Everything because of the afterlife and nothing because its only temporary. A mere blip on our soul's journey.

Keep life simple. Don't get outstretched with all the lame everything's of this world.

Cherish your loved ones.

Time is Everything. Money is Nothing.

Love conquers ALL.

You REALLY can achieve anything.

Don't be a coward.

Fight to the last breath.

Make everything around you "right" all the time. Because you never know what can happen.

Don't hold on to hate and anger. They take you down dangerous roads you don't want or need to be on.

Be compassionate. Be kind. Be loving. But never soft.

Be purposeful.

Be sober.

Have faith.

~*~

Faith.

Faith is believing in something that can't be proven.

Faith is just that, faith.

Faith as defined in *Merriam-Webster* is (1) allegiance to duty or a person, (2) belief and trust in and loyalty to God, (3) firm belief in something for which there is no proof, (4) something that is believed especially with strong conviction.

Having a stronger faith now because I have to, not because I want to, but I NEED to. A belief my baby daughter is in heaven, having faith in that single belief leads me, drives me to want to lead a good life for her so we can be reunited.

Doubting Thomas (John 20:29)

Jesus said to him, "Have you come to believe because you have seen me? Blessed are those who have not seen and have believed."

~*~

3:00 a.m., Spirit hour. They say the veil between this world and the next is the thinnest during this time. Making it possible for spirits to "crossover" and be in this world.

I'm about to be done writing and I look at the clock having no clue what time it is and see it's 3:54 a.m. Spirit hour. Unbelievable. No wonder I awoke and felt compelled to write. Maybe that's why bars close at 2:00 a.m., because there's some spirits they're trying to keep out?

July 15, 2016

I know even in my complete and total sobriety, time will eventually rob me "the feeling" of my daughter in my arms just like time erases everything else. Time doesn't heal, time only erases and moves us further from our original spot. Time is the form of the "blue pill" we are all forced to swallow. I choose the red pill. I choose reality no matter how harsh and cold it seems. It's real. And I don't want to numb that. I don't want to numb the pain. I want to hold onto all the experience and realness. Because she's there, my beautiful baby girl. Love heals. Faith heals. Not time.

~*~

There's no easy way out. Some feelings never die.

July 16, 2016

As I stand, eyes full of tears of sorrow, wiping down my daughter's grave flower pots, I just want them to look nice for her, I want it all to look good for her. Everything perfect. That's all I can do now. It hurts so badly. I feel so helpless and useless. What kind of father am I?

~*~

To myself:
It's ALL your fault. *You* can make up any excuses you want. But it's your entire fault. *You* could've saved her. *You* could've saved her and you didn't. *You* could've done more. Done something. Done anything. *You* did NOTHING. *You* could've saved her and you didn't.
I hate you.

July 17, 2016

Hummingbirds

The four of us at the cemetery together, well, actually, the boys were sleeping in the car. April and I are at Ashlyn's grave talking to each other and blaming ourselves for what happened. Gavin gets out and comes down to the grave, and I ask him if Ryan's awake. He says, "Yes." So, April says she'll go get him. While she's gone I tell Gavin I'm sorry (sorry for his sister passing away as this is his first time at the cemetery). April at this time brings back Ryan. We stand there for some time. I'm holding Ryan and all of us are looking down at the grave.

Gavin says, "Do you think he (Ryan) can see ghosts?"

I, not feeling like it's the appropriate time for this kind of talk cautiously reply, "Spirits? I don't know if he can see spirits, but I can tell you after your baby sister passed away he (Ryan) kept saying baby, baby, baby, and I even asked him where's baby at when we were sitting on the front porch together about a week after it happened and he pointed all over the sky with a big smile on his face."

Gavin says, "Should we ask him now?"

I cautiously answer, "Sure. Ryan where's baby at?"

He looks down at her grave, turns and looks me right in the eyes and says, "Ashlyn."

We pause and April and I exchange glances at each other in a very confused and shocked look like did we just hear what we think we heard? Now keeping in mind Ryan's only fifteen months old at the time.

Ryan again says louder the second time, plain as day, "Ashlyn."

April and I both start crying and I walk with Ryan to the front of her grave and he says "Ashlyn" again just then April starts freaking out saying, "Oh my God, look!"

We see a hummingbird moth flew into Ashlyn's flowers and the hummingbird moth stuck around for a solid minute pollinating all the flowers, which felt like an eternity as we all stood there stunned and amazed. The hummingbird flies away right past my left shoulder and flies up a few rows to some other flowers, but only for a few seconds before it flies straight back down to Ashlyn's flowers for a second time for about five seconds then the hummingbird takes off and flies a loop around encircling us four and flies back off to the same grave it just came from.

July 18, 2016

I can see that now. That look in people's eyes that have felt deep hurt, lost loved ones. That one-thousand-yard stare into the fiery depths of hell and nothingness.

~*~

I need to become emotionally healthy. It's like our (April and I) highways of thought are destroyed and need repair like a gaping wound in the chest.

"Emotional and psychological trauma is the result of extraordinarily stressful events that shatter your sense of security, making you feel helpless in a dangerous world. Traumatic experiences often involve a threat to life or safety, but any situation that leaves you feeling overwhelmed and isolated can be traumatic, even if it doesn't involve physical harm. It's not the objective facts that determine whether an event is traumatic, but your subjective emotional experience of the event. The more frightened and helpless you feel, the more likely you are to be traumatized." (Helpguide.com).

Emotional Trauma can stem from a traumatic event like severe breakup or divorce, natural disasters, acts of war, severe injury, *sudden death of a loved one,* diagnosed life threatening condition of self or loved one, abuse, and many more.

Signs and symptoms of emotional trauma relating to cognitive problems include but not limited to, nightmares, intrusive thoughts from out of the blue, visual mental images of event, loss of memory or concentration, disorientation, confusion, and mood swings.

Victims of Emotional Trauma avoid activities that trigger the event. Also, they have social withdrawal and isolation, depression, and lack of interest in previously enjoyed activities.

Physically the victims can feel easily started, tachycardia, insomnia, edginess, severe exhaustion, changes in eating habits, sexual dysfunction, and extreme alertness always on the 'edge of their seat' looking out for danger. (www.cascadebh.com).

Personally, I've experienced many of these signs and symptoms following my daughter's passing. Cognitively, my mind was in pieces. I lost all ability to concentrate and hold focus. Everything took me four times longer than before as a slowly tried to progress through every daily routine task. I constantly replayed the June 20 day and the days leading up to that day over and over again in my mind. What happened? How could I have done things differently? How did this happen? Why did it happen to me? Did it happen? (Denial) I found myself crying almost instantly sometimes at will various times throughout the day. My mood was always flat or down, never up.

Behaviorally, I withdrew, socially, I deactivated my Facebook account not out of malice, but I just didn't have the time, energy, or interest in keeping up with Facebook communications so rather than looking like I was ignoring anyone I just deactivated it altogether. I apologize to anyone this may have offended. Hobbies and activities couldn't hold my interest either. I found myself blankly staring at the TV screen or wall often many times. Fishing was really the only thing that interested me, which I found interesting because Jesus's apostles were fishermen.

Physically, I had insomnia. I never slept a restful night. Only a few hours here or there, I knew it wasn't restful because I'd wake up feeling more tired than when I went to bed. There were no dreams either, so nightmares were a non-issue. They just didn't exist. Any sexual dysfunction was due to a complete lack of interest in that department, as it seemed such a trivial thing anymore.

Psychologically, I was filled with a lot of disbelief and guilt, which led to a deep dark depression. Often filled with either bouts of anger and sadness. I never considered being one who experienced much anxiety or anxiousness but now I know what it means to have these conditions. I am in a constant anxious state not sure what to do with myself from one moment to the next.

I knew something had to be done. I needed help. If I hung on to any old-time pride I would only damage myself even further. I activated the support structures surrounding me, some already in place and some newly discovered. I am blessed with amazing family and friends that have helped out tremendously with their constant love and support. I also sought out the help of professionals. A licensed practicing counselor truly helped my wife and me in a big way. We would meet with her regularly once a week. I also met a wonderful psychic medium who practices access consciousness which helps ease the mind and change your outlook into a positive one. I would see her every two to three weeks. It's all about whatever works for you, spending time with friends, family, or professionals. The important thing to remember is that you're not alone, so don't think you can face it on your own, because you can't.

~*~

To my wife:

You are my rock. You are the strongest person I know. You are stronger than I ever could be. I love you.

~*~

Ashlyn, I sit here and I write and I write and I write. I don't know how else to get close to you. I wish so badly I could reach out and touch your face.

July 20, 2016

I come home from work late at night and I go to your room hoping to see a cute little dark-haired baby laying there peacefully asleep like I've just been awoken from a terrible, terrible nightmare or a mental disorder I just snapped out of, but I walk into your room and see the empty cold crib and it rips my heart out of my chest. You should be here. My throat swells and my eyes moisten. I collapse into the side of the crib barely able to hold myself up. I miss you so much.

July 21, 2016

It's been a month now after you're gone and I'm still writing thank-you notes to people who showed they cared. Maybe it was them attempting to remove any guilt from the tragedy of saying nothing at all or maybe it was a genuine heartfelt card of sympathy. Whatever the reason I took the opportunity to share you with the rest of the world, because of all the beauty you had to offer. I wanted to share your beauty. I miss you, sweetheart.

~*~

My daughter is forever frozen in time.

~*~

There are things worse in this world than death.

~*~

THE MINE:
While this place has fed everyone, it has also taken everything away.

~*~

TO SELF:
Above all, Andy, I hate you.

July 25, 2016

My day was ruined when I woke up this morning.

July 26, 2016

It's been over a month and I can still feel you in my arms. I can still picture your beautiful face like it was right in front of me. It's been over a month and the pain is still there.

~*~

Words cannot explain what we went through but I'll try my best.

July 28, 2016

Denial

I just don't understand why she's not here. It feels so strange. I can't accept it, and it's tearing me apart inside.

July 29, 2016

I'll never be the same...
AND I don't want to be.

August 4, 2016

The chapter of Ashlyn will never be closed. It will always remain open.
Love you, baby girl.

August 6, 2016

So, I just patiently wait. Patiently wait for your arrival. So excited for the first time I'd meet you and hold you in my arms. Not knowing the first time I laid eyes on you would be our last day together. I love you so much, baby girl. I'm so sorry. I miss you.

August 15, 2016

We know the truth. We know the truth. We know the truth. We know the truth. We know the truth. We know truth. We know truth. We know truth. We know truth.

~*~

The doctors called us and informed us the cord blood clotting reports had come back negative. Ashlyn didn't pass away from a cord issue. We were lied to and led to believe that lie.

August 26, 2016

She has made me stronger than I ever have been before. I pity my enemies.

~*~

The thing I treasure most in my life cannot be taken away.

September 13, 2016

I'm trying to hold onto her as much as I can but time is ripping her out of my arms. As the memory fades away...

My baby girl is in heaven and I hold onto that belief. I know she's there. The hummingbirds told me.

It doesn't change the fact that I miss her so much and I'm still crazy about her.

September 20, 2016

To Ashlyn, I will never forget you. I try to hold onto the "feeling" of you in my arms.

She was so beautiful.
She was so perfect.
AND she was gone…
She is so beautiful.
She is so perfect.
AND she is gone…

It's not easy to walk in these shoes. I think about her all the time. Constantly replaying everything in my mind in an effort to hold onto her.

I'm scared to write this book.

I'm scared to let you (Ashlyn) down.

I'm scared it won't be perfect, like you.

The pain is REAL. It will never stop. Never stop missing her. NEVER.

~*~

If any shred of paranormal exists, then it ALL has a chance to exist.

~*~

I don't want to drink. I don't want everything to just go back to the way things were. It's bad enough that the sun still rises in the east and sets in the west. It's bad enough I'm still back at the same job, etc.

~*~

It's the empty crib that kills me, that tears me up inside. I put together her crib, I put together her dresser. I put together her rocking chair. My wife delicately decorated her room. We had new carpet installed. We painted the room together and dreamed big dreams. Everything was perfect. Everything was ready for her. We *were* very excited. It's the empty crib that hurts.

September 30, 2016

I haven't been in her (Ashlyn) room in a while. I can't even remember the last time. I think today I will. The pain is still there. The image of the empty crib burning into my eyes hits my chest like a solid cold sledgehammer. I can almost hear the thud as it crushes into the center of my chest, caving in all my ribs with a sickly crunching sound. And I weep, I weep for me. I weep for a father without his daughter. This is not how I imagined her childhood would begin with an empty crib and a quiet dark silent stillroom. But going into her room feels much worse than that, it's like a thousand hands around my throat choking me, squeezing the life out of me as my eyes swell up with tears and my nose fills with snot. I lie in the middle of the room and look around at her pictures. Her hair ties. Her furniture. Everything is too much to bear. I get up and open her closet door. Inside I find her bassinet, which I had forgotten we stored in there. The vision of it is equally crushing as the rest of the room if not more. That bassinet was meant for her to sleep peacefully in our room, next to our bedside, not stowed away in this cold closet. Cold just like when I kissed Ashlyn's forehead as she laid in her casket at the funeral home. My eyes pour with tears and it's almost too difficult to see anything now. It's been 102 days without her and I still feel the same. That is comforting. I feel I'm beating time. Ashlyn is timeless. She was real just like how this pain now is real. She's in heaven. She has to be. If she's not, then I don't want to be either.

October 25, 2016

The pain. The pain is real. And I don't try to avoid it, to run from it or push the pain away. I embrace the pain. I let the pain consume me and I wrap myself in it. For if the pain is real then so is my daughter. She is real too. It's all too easy to let the mind fade and her feel like it was a dream, a nightmare, and a distant memory. But it's not, it's real. I know because the pain is real. I remember. I embrace the pain.

November 26, 2016

Her story may have ended with everyone else but it didn't end with me. It only began.

November 28, 2016

I'd be lying if I said I wasn't hoping there was some way to bring her back and this (having a baby) was a way (I feel) to bring her back, but that's not fair to her little sister and that's not fair to her. She's in heaven, she's in God's glory, why would I want to take her from such as beautiful place? A place my human mind can't even begin to imagine.

December 8, 2016

Lord you may not <u>need</u> me, but I <u>NEED</u> you.

_*_

Life is too short. More often than not, when people are confronted with bad times, they say life is too short then they quickly forget and go back living the same way they were before.

December 10, 2016

I think about you every day, baby girl. There's not an hour that goes by without you on my mind. I can't look at a baby without seeing you, seeing your gorgeous face and thick dark hair. The memory of you is a love-filled one, but there is also a lot of pain because you're not here.

The love and pain I feel for you are real and intense. I embrace them both. For they both remind me I have a daughter, she is perfect and her name is Ashlyn.

The feeling of meeting my daughter for the first time and knowing she was already gone was beyond any words this world can express, so I'm not even going to attempt to begin to describe to you the tidal wave of emotion.

December 24, 2016

We visited Ashlyn's grave and brought her two poinsettia plants. I miss you so much, baby girl. Merry Christmas.

December 25, 2016

We bring her the hummingbird musical snow globe we got from her uncle Jimmy and play it for her.

December 26, 2016

I do imagine my wife and I's first baby was a girl and she and Ashlyn's souls are happily together with each other giggling, smiling, and playing in Heaven.

Actually, it's not really imagining, it's a very strong feeling I have that that is certainly true and a vision of them dance in my head and one day, when I leave this tormented world, I'll be reunited with my two girls. That's why I got to be good. That's why I have to do God's work while I'm here. Be a good person and be a shining example of God's love and faith.

~*~

It's her day every day. Every day is JUNE 20. NEVER FORGET THE FEELING.

January 25, 2017

She (Ashlyn) taught me how to celebrate life. How to stop being a coward.

January 26, 2017

I feel that something is coming. Something greater.

Hummingbirds are seen almost daily and we're in the middle of winter.

Today I spotted a hummingbird on Grandma's sweater in a photo of my dad and grandma. I never noticed it, but the photograph has been sitting out in my parent's house for almost a year. Now the hummingbird on my grandma's shirt is as big as a billboard. I showed the photograph to my mother and she said, "Oh my God. There is a hummingbird." A redheaded Irish Catholic in my family, my grandma was revered as close to a saintlike person I've ever met with her modest, humble, and very giving nature. Surely, this sign was heaven sent and I felt my daughter, Ashlyn, and my grandma must be happy together in a place no human can even dream of.

The hummingbird reports came pouring in from friends and family across the state of Pennsylvania. Maybe everyone heard what they meant to us or maybe everyone was just looking for them, or maybe the hummingbird sightings were something more, a sign from up above.

I feel a strong connection to her, my daughter Ashlyn. My soul yearns to be with her. That's why I think my earthly body is saddened with such grief because physically here on earth we'll never be together, but my soul is hopeful and joyous with the faith our two souls will be reunited again.

I feel closest to her than I do with anyone I've ever known.

January 27, 2017

Ryan always says two. Ryan born on April 7, 2015. Ashlyn born June 20, 2016 and Cameron March 1, 2013.

When I begin to put the pieces together, I realize it all fits together. Everything is connected to each other. Ryan... Ashlyn... all of it.

~*~

It is our conscious, our mind that is a gift from a higher power.
I'm awake and my eyes are open.
You're awake, but are your eyes closed?

~*~

On Christmas Day we brought to Ashlyn's grave a humming-bird musical snow globe, winded it up and played a song for her. I asked her to keep the hummingbirds coming (now it's December, winter time in Pennsylvania) but it made no difference, the hummingbirds kept coming almost daily. Whether it is a card from a family member or friend. A pair of leggings with hummingbirds on them from an old friend or a hummingbird jewelry pin belonging once to my grandma sent to us from my aunt. The hummingbirds are everywhere. It's a beautiful comforting sign to see. We miss her so much, but it's good to know she is with us, watching us, and she's okay.

February 1, 2017

She's the most beautiful baby. I want to share her with the world.
Writing is a way to hang on to the feelings and experiences I've had with her, to hang on to her. It seems all too easy, time changes the memories into a bubble dreamlike state. The writing makes it tangible, makes it more real. By writing I feel I'm able to hold onto her a bit more even if the memories are filled with pain. Pain is all I have left.
And a few curls of her beautiful hair.

February 2, 2017

It's easy to grab a cold one and have a "screw it" attitude, but I don't want to be that way anymore. She's changed me forever. I confront all of my problems head on, and take care of what needs done.
I don't drink right now because I'm going through some tough times and I cannot afford to be hindered in any way. Plus, I don't

want to "turn the page" or go back to the way things were like she never happened.

February 6, 2017

And you wonder if the lady you see at the cemetery is a grandmother coming to her grandchild, then you realize things aren't what they appear, and how inaccurate that assessment is. She's not actually a grandmother visiting a grandchild, but a mother visiting her child that has passed back in 1974. Forty-three years later, she's still a mother. A mother in mourning and her soul still cries out for her lost child. It's very sad. That grief, that pain that child is never gone but that's okay, that's a good feeling, because the love always remains for that baby. Love conquers ALL. Even Death.

February 9, 2017

Because the past is the past and it cannot be unwritten and in order for us to find happiness in this world we must find ourselves to be healthy spiritually because it's not the world or anything in it that will make us happy but it's ourselves within ourselves that'll make us happy I feel.

~*~

These are not ideas I'm thinking of writing but feelings straight from the heart. If I don't put them out there in the universe, write them down on paper, my soul will explode and burst.

February 10, 2017

Ryan asking for a pink balloon makes me think he's asking for Ashlyn because we have no pink balloons, only blue ones and yellow ones from his first birthday party.

_*_

I'm sitting there with my wife watching some television show with both boys sound asleep in bed. Out of nowhere the "love to learn" Elmo begins talking. Now I had already cleaned the room up for the night and I had specifically closed Elmo's mouth and set him on my son's recliner for the night. Our spiritual teacher told us these things would happen, toys would go off for no reason or you might catch something out of the corner of your eye. She told us not to ignore them as faulty engineering or your mind playing tricks on you, but even still I ignored Elmo as my logical mind kicked in proclaiming it must have low batteries and brushed it off and just as I finished that thought the "feed me" dinosaur began talking from the toy chest. "Can you feed me the purple grapes?" My logic quickly vanished as I realized what was going on and my spiritual teacher's words echoed inside my head. "Pay attention to the signs. Your daughter is with you and she will try to contact you." Purple was the color I saw for Ashlyn. My eyes welled up with tears and my wife got up from the couch, without saying a word walked over to the baby monitor. I said, "What are you doing?" She didn't respond and picked up the monitor. I got up and joined my wife watching the screen and to our disbelief there was a wispy orb fluttering around our son in the baby monitor screen. I said, "Oh my God, it's Ashlyn. Is this really happening?" My wife and I both were crying now as we watched the wispy orb dance around the screen as if to say, "Hi Mom and Dad, I love you and I'm with you and I'm with my big brother too."

February 14, 2017

We (the family) visit Ashlyn's grave. My wife hates calling it a grave, because she feels it's too cold. And I must say it is, but it's where the body of my beautiful daughter now rests. Our one-year-old son, Ryan, is with us. He's happy as usual, he runs around and finds a few places where water has collected on the ground creating little mud puddles. It's a very surreal feeling, standing there in front of my daughter's place of rest while Ryan happily runs and giggles along. It doesn't feel real. We place flowers on her headstone. Red flowers in recognition of Valentine's Day. Oh, you're my sweet valentine, Ashlyn. I wish I could kiss your little forehead and hold you in my arms again. I walk over to where Ryan is playing and pick him up before he gets too muddy. My wife and I both exchange somber looks toward one another as we look into the bright blue life filled eyes of little happy innocent Ryan, not knowing that his little sister is gone. We both say, "Ryan, say Love you Sissy." Instead Ryan lovingly smiles at Ashlyn's place of rest and says, "HI." Maybe he knows more than we think.

~*~

We are all still searching for something. Answers? Questions? Someone?

We are ALL searching for something.

February 15, 2017

Big News

My wife today had a doctor's appointment to diagnose feminine problems she was having. She called me while at the doctor's office and said the unthinkable, "Andy, I'm pregnant." I was in shock. Total disbelief shock. I couldn't believe it. We've been blessed.

The previous few days were very strange. I felt very strange. My soul must have known before my body did. I was overcome with such great joy and I couldn't place a finger on why, and now I know exactly why. Ashlyn's little brother or sister was here. They've arrived. Our little rainbow baby. (A rainbow baby is a term given to babies that have come after a loss.) I don't like thinking of Ashlyn Marie as a loss for she is my daughter. She will always be my daughter and one day we'll be beautifully reunited, but the experience was a loss. In this world, in this life, it was a loss. A great tragic loss.

It's difficult and a selfish feeling to have, to desire one particular gender over another but I can't help feeling one way or another. Of course, I'm happy and excited and above all want a happy healthy baby. Who doesn't? But when I think about the gender and what the baby may be, if the baby was a girl then I feel a wave of mixed emotions. Happy that Ashlyn's little sister will enjoy and share her room. Sad because I can't help feeling it's really turning a page in a chapter in my life that I want to remain open and sad because a baby girl would almost feel like she's "replacing" Ashlyn and that feeling hurts, for I never, never want Ashlyn to feel replaced EVER.

If the baby were a boy, then I feel I would only be naturally happy and excited. Another little boy to roughhouse and a little brother Ryan could take under his wing. They are best buds for life and we could remain Ashlyn's room intact just how it is for her, while we remodeled the new room for our baby boy to come. It's selfish I know, but I can't help that's just how I feel. What can I say? Ashlyn has me wrapped around her little finger and she always will.

February 16, 2017

I read my letter to Ashlyn, my daughter, at her funeral service at the cemetery. I read it aloud in front of my wife and I's immediate families, choked up, sobbing through a wall of tears…

June 23, 2016

Dear Ashlyn,

First, you're the most beautiful baby I ever seen. I try to make sense of things and I can't. I don't know why things are, but what I do know is I had a daughter whom I loved very much, even before I laid eyes on you, you had me wrapped around your little finger, but you're gone now and my heart is broken, but that doesn't change the love I have for you. I have to keep the faith and a priest told me God needs little angels. I'm not sure why he does, but I know you're in a better place and that comforts me. I won't be strong without you here, God will have to carry me, so let God know that since your up there.
You can bother me anytime you want.
And until we meet again...
Love forever and always,
Your Daddy

February 17, 2017

We have a spiritual teacher/healer that told us, "Your daughter will try and contact you from time to time to let you know she's here. If you hear toys going off or catch something out of the corner of your eye, you hear daddy or mommy and your son is sound asleep, know that is your daughter and she's letting you know she's with you."

Ashlyn is the glue that holds me together. She makes me want to be a better person, to be someone she'd be proud to call her father.

~*~

If you heal your spirit, you can heal your body and mind.

February 19, 2017

When you look in the mirror and see someone staring back at you, that soul staring back into your soul. You know that we've been through a lot together and my heart cries out for that poor man's soul and there's also a mutual respect and understanding there. It's not in a narcissist way but in a look of acknowledgement that the guy in the mirror and I have been through a lot together, a lot of ups and downs, and I'm astonished we made it.

February 21, 2017

It's like every day I find myself with him (Ryan). I turn to look but she's not there and in my mind it screams, "Why is she not here?" My soul begins to ache, sorrow hits me hard for she (Ashlyn) looked just like him, Ryan.

Countless number of tears I've shed writing her (Ashlyn's) journal. My throat seals shut, tears flow and it's difficult to breath. I'm lost without her. I can feel myself aging by the minute. Not that I care about that anymore.

February 22, 2017

Come back to me…

February 27, 2017

In life, it's okay I can handle anything. I've stared into the gates of hell.

~*~

April, I love you, I love you so much, and you are so strong because you're having another baby and even though we could lose this baby, you're willing to start this journey, because you wanted her (Ashlyn). You've always wanted her. And we still do. She was a heavenly surprise when we first knew she was here. We miss you, baby girl.

~*~

I feel like I've been dead. All my life. I haven't experienced much of anything. I feel alive now, equipped with a full awareness of the world around me.

March 3, 2017

Life is a journey. A search for answers to our questions, whatever they may be.

If you don't care to find the answer to a question, then there is no motivation.

If you ask the question or live the question and always have the answer then that is being alive, this is how and why experts are made.

Because they relish in the fact that they are experts in their given field and that causes them to really enjoy life and enjoy their careers.

What do you want to be an expert of? What comes naturally "easy" to you? Because what comes easy to you shouldn't go ignored, just because it comes naturally easy to you doesn't mean it comes easy for others. It comes easy because there lies your strength and it's what you're good at. What's your passion? What motivates you? What gets you going? What questions burn at the center of your soul?

March 4, 2017

And we will never know the answers to the questions that we seek. Why did she have to die? Why can't we be together? Why is she not here? There's questions which cannot be answered but take comfort in knowing that this is not the end but the beginning of something greater and until we meet again, may the Lord hold you in the palm of his hand.

May the Road Rise to meet you.
May the Wind always be at your back.
May the Sun shine warm upon your face.
May the Rain fall soft on your fields.
And until we meet again, may the Lord hold you in the palm of his hand.
~ Irish Blessing

March 5, 2017

My mind isn't right. It doesn't feel right. It's been nine months since my baby girl has gone away and I can still feel the remnants of the emotional trauma. It's like I'm trying to reboot a computer and recover the data, which was lost. Everything processes slow, so very slow. Slowly the mind recovers like the body would after a horrific injury.

I try to string life events together in my mind in an effort to recover what was lost and there are only fragments of memory left in a large vast of empty space.

I try to connect the dots with tragic events. Grandpa sitting in his recliner stricken from cancer laying on the couch unbeknownst to me, as I was only four years old, of his deteriorating health condition due to lung cancer. He would give out "granddollars" on Sundays and was always happy. Sometimes tired but over all I remember him being very happy and loving, but then he's gone and there's blankness there. I remember he's gone and I'm talking with my cousin, Timmy, on the stairs, at Grandpa's house. I was sitting about halfway up the stairs and Timmy was sitting on a step a few higher than me. Next memory after that is my parents walking up the stairs to my brother and I's bedroom to tell us that Samson, our first family dog, had cancer and was going to pass away soon. They said he was very sick. I hate cancer. It takes everything away—my grandpa, our family dog. After this memory is blankness for a while.

I haven't been drinking, I'm too worn down for that. I'm too much in recovery, I feel alive and don't what anything numbing me or holding me back from my peak potential. I write down and keep track of my daily activity. I take "IQ" pills though, they're most likely a hoax. It's all in an attempt to recover or save my brain.

March 6, 2017

I don't know if this experience is unique to myself, something inside tells me it's not but for the longest time following my daughter's passing away I would wake up at exactly three o' clock in the morning. I had a lot of restless nights but as always from three to four I'd be wide awake, bright-eyed, and bushy-tailed as the saying goes. I even went as far as to screenshot my phone one night when I found myself immediately awoken at 3:00 a.m. From time to time I still feel this way waking up at 3:00 a.m. Now it has been about nine months since she's passed away, but I feel like I should start setting my alarm clock for 3:00 a.m. because it's during this hour I feel motivated and I could write in Ashlyn's journal at this time frame as motivation, maybe she's talking to me, through me, helping and guiding me.

~*~

My body is depressed without her.
My mind is obsessed with her.
My soul longs for her.

March 9, 2017

I'm so happy because I know she, her soul, exists but yet I still remain deadlocked in total sadness because she physically is not with me now in this lifetime. There'll be no laughs shared, no tickling, no giggles, no tea parties, no smiles exchanged, no hugs, no kisses. Oh, how I long to see her again, to hold her in my arms, to kiss her rosy cheeks, to smell her hair, to just… see her again.

She has given us an amazing gift. A gift of faith, a gift of love.

March 10, 2017

My wife's doctor's appointment for the new baby. The first ultrasound to see the baby's heartbeat and find out the due date. Would you believe that our doctor had a blouse on covered in a tessellation of hummingbirds? Hummingbirds! All over her blouse. She had no idea about what hummingbirds symbolized to my wife and me. We kept this to ourselves as to not startle the lady but crazy! Ashlyn sends us signs everywhere. It was almost as if to say, "Hi, I'm here with you and I'm excited about my new little brother or sister!" It's winter in the north and we see hummingbirds everywhere.

March 13, 2017

And now we've just received the news on February 15 that my wife and I have been blessed with another child. We're both very happy and elated, but my wife is filled with great anxiety and understandably so. So, she asks me, "Is everything going to be all right?" I say, "Yes, of course it will be. Don't worry. Worrying won't do you any good." But how can I say that? When we've already been through so much and experienced two losses before? Our first baby miscarried and Ashlyn passed away. So, I change my tune because the truth is I don't know if everything will be all right. Only God knows. Whatever will be will be. Embrace the now with hope and love, not fear and despair. May the God of hope fill you with all joy and peace in believing, so that by the power of the Holy Spirit you may abound in hope. (Romans 15:13). The fact is we've been blessed with Ashlyn's little brother or sister and we're ALL in this together. ALL of it.

_*_

It's been nine months since she's been gone and I still feel the same way about her. Completely and utterly obsessed and infatuated. She's my little angel. Oh, how my heart and soul aches to be with her. She's constantly on my mind. Though sadly she's not talked about as much these days as she was in the past, but consciously she's right there in my mind, all the time.

~*~

There was a great anxiety going back to work. How was I to communicate with people? How was I to care? To give a damn? And to think this way can be extremely dangerous and reckless in my line of work, but I work with a lot of intelligent, caring human beings who were quick to embrace me back into the workforce and pour their hearts out with stories of their own experiences or family member's experiences they've been involved with. One person's story of miscarriage, another's stillborn, another's story of SIDS. It's the crosses that we bear through life, like spiritual soldiers, they define us.

March 14, 2017

They say that cats can sense things, that they are hypersensitive. They can sense things others cannot. Things like the "otherworld" or spirits, etc. I believe this is true because since my dear daughter, Ashlyn, passed away, my three cats have been sleeping in front of her bedroom door and they never slept in front of her bedroom door prior to her passing.

~*~

This book represents one year of "rough draft" writing about my feelings and actions, about my soul, about my daughter, about how I feel about everything. All outside sources and research was done after the year without her. I didn't want this journal to turn into a research paper and it probably would have. I really wanted to nail down how I really felt. I wanted to make the book for her and capture the feeling and make it as close to real as possible so that I could have it forever sealed inside this book. I didn't want the book bogged down with research and outside sources. I wanted it to become something I could cherish forever as a tribute to my greatest love, Ashlyn.

March 16, 2017

Tonight I've decided that every dollar, if any, that I make off selling *Ashlyn's Journal* will be donated to the "stillborn stillloved" charity. I decided this while I was writing *Ashlyn's Journal* after hours. Just when I was about to sleep tonight I took my sweatshirt off got into bed and in that very instant Ryan's nighttime sleepy sound aquarium started playing by itself in his room. I knew this because as soon as I heard it I clicked the baby monitor screen on expecting to see Ryan sitting up or at least stirring in his crib but he wasn't, he was perfectly silent, peacefully sleeping. I know it's her. I know she's here with me, and I know she's proud of her daddy.

March 19, 2017

Why Is She Your Greatest Love?

Because there was so much loss there. So much hopes and dreams I've had for you and they were gone, ripped away from me and in that tragic end there was a great love that burrowed its way deep, deep down inside me, inside my soul. It was a complete obsession, and still is, Ashlyn, my greatest love.

⁓*⁓

I wish I could say everything is okay now, that everything is better. All the experiences I've endured have made me see the light and I'm relieved and happy now but the truth is I'm obsessed. Obsessed with that Thursday, four days before she passed away. I know the past is the past and it can't be unwritten, but if only time travel were real I'd go back to that day and make everything right. I WOULD NOT LEAVE THAT HOSPITAL! I WOULD DEMAND THEY…

sobs… Ashlyn would be here and all my wife's tears would be washed away, never to happen. All that heartbreak gone. I'll never stop obsessing over that day, so if anyone has the ability to travel back in time please let me know.

March 20, 2017

Today is the first day of Spring. You passed away, or gone to heaven as your grandpa more commonly known as Pappy prefers to say, on the first day of summer. So, three seasons have now passed by since I saw your sweet, angelic face. It feels like it's been thirty years and yesterday all at once.

The feeling is like a void that can never be filled. A longing, it's like the experiences of people losing their arms in a tragic accident. They know their arm was there, they can feel it, but it's gone. Losing her feels like I lost an arm or definitely a big piece of me is lost. A part I can't get back.

~*~

Part of the message learned sadly is don't trust people no matter what credentials they hold, because at the end of the day (and the beginning), they're all only human. Trust your intuition. Trust your gut. Your primal instincts have been sharpened for thousands of years and they are to be listened to, not ignored and silenced. After all, it was our primal instincts that got the human race this far on this blue marble spinning endlessly through dark space. The opposable thumbs helped too.

March 21, 2017

Trying to live when I'm standing on the edge…

March 26, 2017

Your perception of life changes when the one you want to be with the most is no longer here on Earth.

You begin to question *everything.*

What are we *really* doing here?

What is the *purpose?*

What is *our* purpose?

My heart aches for her…

March 28, 2017

I truly believe trust no one, love everyone. Even Dr. X, I'm sorry we had to be placed in such grievance circumstances. I desperately wish things would've turned out better for all of us.

I mistakenly placed my trust in you, and for that I'm angry with myself, but I know the outcome was never your intention, but my eyes are open now. I understand.

March 31, 2017

I pondered deeply on how am I making it? How am I making it through this? I don't know how I am. Then it struck me. I'm __not__ really making it. God is carrying me through all of this. *We're* making it. I've given myself to faith and God is carrying me through like footprints in the sand.

One night I dreamed I was walking along the beach with the Lord. Many scenes from my life flashed across the sky. In each scene I noticed footprints in the sand. Sometimes there were two sets of footprints, other times there were one set of footprints. This bothered me because I noticed that during the low periods of my life, when I was suffering from anguish, sorrow, or defeat, I could see only one set of footprints.

So I said to the Lord, "You promised me Lord, that if I followed you, you would walk with me always. But I have noticed that during the most trying periods of my life there have only been one set of foot-

prints in the sand. Why, when I needed you most, you have not been there for me?"

The Lord replied, "The times when you have seen only one set of footprints, is when I carried you."

~ Mary Stevenson

April 5, 2017

God is good. We've been blessed with another child. Ashlyn's little brother or sister. I get to meet Ashlyn's little brother or sister. Do you know how lucky and honored that makes me feel? I'm a very blessed man.

April 7, 2017

When I drive to work, when I'm at a restaurant. She's all I think about I'm truly obsessed.

April 8, 2017

People ask me how are you doing? Or how's your wife? How's the two of you doing? And I say good but I feel guilty saying good because it feels like I'm moving on, moving away from her and that I don't care. I don't want to move away. If I say not good, then I feel guilty because it feels like I'm looking for pity or sympathy. The truth is I don't know if I'm "good" anymore. What is "good?" I don't even know what is "good." All I can say is each day I try to get better and BE better.

April 10, 2017

So we found out what we're having today and it's a girl! We cried so hard together when my wife and I found out. We're so happy. Ashlyn will never be replaced first and foremost. This little baby, this little girl, this bundle of joy I truly feel is a gift from God, grows our family larger. Ashlyn will always be a part of our family. We prepared a room for a little girl. We prepared a room for Ashlyn. This didn't come to fruition. Ashlyn didn't get to come home. But hopefully Ashlyn's little sister, Alexis, can. We've decided to name her Alexis. Alexis Marie, she'll share the same middle name and the same initials as her big sis, Ashlyn Marie. They'll also share the same room.

April 13, 2017

FROM KARA, SPIRITUAL HEALER/ PSYCHIC MEDIUM

"Doing better than all of us ever."
"Bigger than you can imagine."
"When you randomly think of her, that's her, she's with you."

April 14, 2017

Thinking back when telling the doctor, I wanted my unborn daughter to be treated just like she's a baby tears my heart to pieces. And my heart goes out to that dad, to that man. Oh, Andy I think that father... that father was me.

~*~

I will always grieve. We always will grieve. And there's absolutely nothing wrong with that.

~*~

"Hi honey, I love you."
"I love you, Daddy."

"What's it like up there?"
"More beautiful than even you could imagine."
"I miss you, honey."
"I miss you too, Daddy. I wish… I wanted to stay but I couldn't."
"I understand."
"I know you do, Daddy. That's why I love you so."

~*~

I feel an overwhelming love coming from her. A love so strong it brings me to tears.

~*~

I don't know why, but I feel so driven and determined for something. I'm not exactly sure what that something is yet.
Answers? Divinity? Truth?

April 17, 2017

On June 20, 2016, my world changed forever, when my daughter passed away and for a long time my head just felt crushed, shattered into pieces.

April 18, 2017

All tests were negative. She was perfect. The only way to find an actual cause of death was an autopsy and at the time this (in our minds) was not even an option. Just the thought of putting my baby girl, even if only her body, through that ripped my heart to even more pieces, but that doesn't mean it's not the right move for you because it most definitely could be the right thing for you and your family.

She's forever changed me. Things will never be the same and in some ways that's a very good thing. She's tapped into the darkest recesses of my soul and has made me the better man I am today.

Words cannot explain what we went through. They can only attempt.

April 22, 2017

I feel such joy. Such great joy and excitement for the things to come.

I feel very hopeful about the future.

My faith in God is stronger than it has ever been.

~*~

Words cannot describe the pain and anguish our family has been through.

My heart pours out for any families having gone through (this). Parents should never outlive their children. We weren't meant to. It's not natural. We're supposed to procreate, pass the torch, teach, nurture, foster, and love our offspring, our little ones.

Such a terrible tragedy, but in that tragedy hope, faith, and love can be found. That's what we must hold on to and BELIEVE.

April 24, 2017

Spiritual Awakening Meeting Dixie

There have been often times when I felt like something was rubbing against my legs like strings or a silky scarf. Every time I felt the sensation I would reach down and brush my ankles off, but every time there was nothing there, no strings, no scarf, no spider webs, nothing. Then one night at our mediation group, Dixie, one newly learned psychic medium that has developed amazing talents said to me, "Andy, do you ever feel like there's a wispy feeling around you? Like going around your legs?" I said shocked, "Yes, I recently felt that so many times." She said, "That's her, that's your daughter trying to get your attention by being playful with you." This put me to tears. How she hit on this new phenomenon I was experiencing was incredible.

April 25, 2017

I've met two psychic mediums. A psychic medium is described in two titles, psychic and medium. A psychic can practice any sort of long list of psychic abilities like clairvoyance the ability to see things that are hidden. Also, intuition the ability to just "know" things without being told. The title medium refers to someone who can receive messages from the spirit world in a variety of ways. I've encountered two very good psychic mediums that were brought to the point of tears after sensing, feeling, experiencing Ashlyn's overwhelming love for me.

Alexis Marie is going to get the best dad ever! And she can thank her big sis, Ashlyn, for that.

April 26, 2017

You should wear your tears, wipe them with your hands, not a tissue. Let them soak into your skin and absorb all the precious beautiful emotion.

May 3, 2017

When you have faith in God, you have nothing to fear.

I have the key. I have the most powerful weapon in the world. Faith. When you have faith in God, *real* faith, your invincible, nothing can stop you or harm you. Nothing.

May 5, 2017

Today is my birthday. I don't really pay much attention to my birthdays anymore, just one more year gone by and one year older, but today I went to visit Ashlyn's grave. I can feel her love all the time, it's constant. Her love is overwhelming. Her love is all consuming.

May 9, 2017

We went to our first essential oil meeting today with wonderful essential oil expert Leslie. April and I walked in, April immediately noticed a hummingbird decoration on the wall. Of course, the sign of a hummingbird carries significant meaning to us, so April points the decoration out to me. I say, "Oh wow, that's awesome." Leslie comes over looking half startled and half spooked. She says, "What?" We tell her, "Oh, you have a hummingbird on your wall and it holds great meaning to us." Leslie almost now to the point of tears says, "What meaning is that?" We tell her our daughter passed away last year and hummingbirds have always come to us as a sign for her. Leslie, teary-eyed now, says that her sister passed away last year and she loved hummingbirds and they, too, come as a sign for her for her sister.

The hummingbird spirit animal symbolizes the enjoyment of life and lightness of being. Those who have the hummingbird as a totem are invited to enjoy the sweetness of life, lift up negativity whenever it creeps in and express love more fully in their daily endeavors. This fascinating bird is capable of the most amazing feats despite its small size, such as traveling great distances or being able to fly backwards. By affinity with the hummingbird, those who have this bird as totem may be encouraged to develop their adaptability and resiliency while keeping a playful and optimistic outlook.

From then on, we had a wonderful discussion and it really set the tone for a beautiful meeting to talk with Leslie about essential oils and just about life in general.

After the appointment we went back to my parents' house where our two-year-old son, Ryan, was being watched/babysat by his

Mom-Mom and Pappy. After some time had passed, Ryan wanted to go out on the deck so we all went out on the deck, after a minute or two April says, "Look! Is that a hummingbird?" We looked at their bird feeder and sitting there for only a moment and then hovering around the bird feeder was indeed a hummingbird, our first hummingbird sighting of the year. It was colored green on its back, white on its belly and around its neck was what looked like a hot pink scarf around its delicate neck.

Later in the afternoon we had our second ultrasound for our second coming daughter, Alexis. At the ultrasound, Alexis was nothing short of stunning. Even at only sixteen weeks old, she was fully developed with perfect features and was even caught sucking her thumb. I half-jokingly asked the technician, "Is it normal for the baby to be that cute this early on?" She humored me and said, "No, your baby is exceptional." We got a laugh out of the exchange and she was very sweet, printing out not one or two pictures but sixteen pictures for us to take home.

Alexis is beautiful and unique in her own way. We're very excited to meet her. Very excited to meet Ashlyn's sister. She's perfect just like Ashlyn.

~*~

I will always be sad for missing Ashlyn. I will always long for her as I'm in human form.

But I will rejoice and celebrate Alexis. She deserves it. Ashlyn would want that too.

~*~

Just stop and listen to the people around you. Listen to their thoughts, their perspectives, their feelings, and emotions. Don't just hurry to get through the conversation, but really pay attention to and delve deep to make deeper connections and with one another. You'll be amazed to find out the beautiful relationships that will begin to be nurtured and grow. An experience that would've sadly passed you up had you just focused on the next thing.

Live in the NOW and the future will take care of itself.

You'll never experience the journey if you're always just focused on where you're going. Enjoy the journey. Somewhere in there is where you'll find true beaming happiness.

˷*˷

I still miss you, Ashlyn, so much. I cry and I cry and I cry. Daddy loves you so much, Baby Girl, so, so much.

May 16, 2017

So, I'm in Hallmark looking for a Mother's Day gift for my wife and I'm looking for something with hummingbirds because I'll practically buy anything that has hummingbirds on it at this point. I look around the whole store and find nothing. I mean nothing. Then I come to the picture frames and I see one silver picture frame with the words engraved "tiny miracle" with a generic picture of an ultrasound shot of a baby. I thought what a perfect frame for Alexis's ultrasound picture, and I look up just as I finished that thought to the shelf above it and guess what I'm staring at—a hummingbird! My jaw drops. A hummingbird on the cover of a children's book staring right back at me. Unbelievable! It was as if Ashlyn was right there saying, "Hi, Daddy, great gift!" I felt such a high level of validation Ashlyn was there with me and wanted me to get the frame and she's happy her little sister, Alexis, is being celebrated and she's on the way. Needless to say, I got the "tiny miracle" picture frame and I also got the children's book with the hummingbird on the cover too. Maybe baby Alexis can read it in the not too distant future.

May 24, 2017

I can feel her presence all the time, this overwhelming feeling of love and compassion. She's with me all the time. Always at the forefront of my mind. I can visualize me holding her in my arms and looking down at her sweet angelic beautiful face. My eyes well up with tears as I look up to the sky while feeling that overwhelming strong love connection between us. She's always right here with me.

May 27, 2017

Our little two-year-old, Ryan is dancing, watching Charlie Brown, the Great Pumpkin. I'm asleep upstairs and my wife is watching Ryan. I'm awoken by my wife calling my name, "Andy! Andy!" As she bolts into our bedroom. I'm awake now startled. "What is it?" I say. She says, "Ryan was dancing watching Charlie Brown when he said Ashlyn is here." I said, "What? What'd he say?" She says, "He said Ashlyn! Ashlyn!" She replied back to him, "Where's Ashlyn?" He pointed right beside himself smiling, and continued dancing.

June 1, 2017

I'm always thinking about you. I'm going to keep on loving you, Ashlyn. No matter how much time passes that love for you will never fade. It's timeless. It's powerful. It's our love.

June 10, 2017

It's been almost one year since you've been gone. You've touched the lives of so many here. Though you never drew a single breath you've done more positive work here on earth than I could do in ten lifetimes. You're such a strong soul. I'm so very proud of you, baby girl, I want you to sincerely know that.

Last year on June 20, 2016, was not the end of your story, Ashlyn, it was only the beginning. I've grown so close to you, closer than anyone I've ever met in my life. I've grown very strong spiritually and that has paved the way and made fertile ground for our beautiful relationship we have together. Even though I can't see you with my earthly eyes I know you're with me always. I can almost reach out and hold you just like I did that day when I first laid eyes on you.

Until we're together my little sweetheart...

June 15, 2017

As the "man" of the household you got to be strong, right? You got to keep it together, right? One has to ask, what *is* strong? Not crying and suppressing your feelings down, bottling them up is not strong. You're only avoiding what's right in front of you, fixing the issue temporarily until it resurfaces again and you push it back down again.

Being strong is having the courage to confront life's issues "head on." To deal with the challenges, no matter how difficult they may seem.

June 18, 2017

You are strong, very strong. You've had an impact on a lot of people's lives, young and old, age does not seem to matter to you, as you are timeless. A very positive impact. I'm honored and so lucky to call you my daughter. I love you dear, baby Ashlyn.

_*_

My wife says I'm a great father to Ashlyn, how am I a great father to her? The same way any good father is to their children, I recognize her existence, I love her, I celebrate her, I don't shield my emotions away from her or about her. I proudly express my great love and feelings for her. I don't stuff her away in a closet because I'm filled with shame, anger, or guilt. I celebrate Ashlyn's life and the gift she was to me and still continues to be. She's changed everything.

She's opened my eyes to what life is really about—Love and Peace. True Love and Peace not only as words in a dictionary but as a way of life, a life worth living.

June 20, 2017

One year ago today, we had five hours with her. We got five hours to be with her. If I can have something to take me back to that day even as horrible as it was, it was still the only day I got to spend with her.

.~*~.

We bought her flowers and a balloon. I mean what am I supposed to get my daughter who's been gone from us for a year now? This was supposed to be her first birthday party, a smash cake, friends and family gathered around, all talking about how cute Ashlyn is and how happy she is. This is not how I envisioned it, standing here in the cemetery bringing flowers to a gravesite. Then at some point you just have to, I just have to stop myself and realize nothing is ever going to be good enough. Nothing. So that's where we stopped, we got her four pots of pink and white flowers, a vase with multi-colored hydrangeas and a Disney princess Happy Birthday balloon.

Happy Birthday, Baby Girl, at least we got to be here and spend this time with you.

.~*~.

I'm happy now because she's with me.

June 24, 2017

What is a parent called after a child passes away? There still is no word. It's not natural.

In October 1988, President Ronald Reagan declared October as National Pregnancy and Infant Loss Awareness Month saying, "When a child loses his parent, they are called an orphan. When a spouse loses her or his partner, they are called a widow or widower. When parents lose their child, there isn't a word to describe them." (October15th.com).

~*~

People have lived entire full lives and have not had as nearly an impact as these babies.

If I add up all the great influencers in my life, the teachers, coaches, priests, friends, etc. they wouldn't add up to one percent of how much Ashlyn has affected me. She's changed everything. She's such a huge part of my life that everything else seems so tiny, so small, so insignificant when you look at the bigger picture, she makes everything so miniscule, so simple and so easy to deal with. She's my rock, the one I turn to. She truly is my angel in heaven. My sweet baby girl angel.

Remembrance Walk, June 24, 2017

One year and four days since she's been gone, and today we walked with other ones who've suffered losses. Stillbirth, miscarriage, SIDS, we walked for them in a remembrance walk. We are hurt. We are a community of people united who have angels watching over us. These angels have touched each and every one of our lives in a very real and profound way. I walk for her. I walk for Ashlyn Marie. My greatest love.

On June 20, a huge part of me died that day and out of the depths of hell and anguish something new was born. Something stronger. Something greater. She has made me stronger. She has opened up my eyes, my heart, and my soul. I owe everything to her and God.

June 25, 2017

To remember her, that transcends all things, all religions, to remember her and that she didn't die in vain but she had a huge impact on the lives she's touched.

~*~

People say, "So sorry for your loss," but I don't view her as a loss but rather I gained, I gained an angel.

Here is a collection of songs I felt drawn to at one point in time in the days, weeks, and months after Ashlyn was gone as I cycled through anger, sadness, and emptiness. I like sad songs because they don't let me forget. I like angry songs because they let me be angry.

Gasoline by Halsey
What Makes Us Girls by Lana Del Rey
See Fire by Jasmine Thompson
Talking Body by Tove Lo
Chandelier by Sia
Habits by Tove Lo (feel like the opposite of this song's lyrics "gotta stay sober so I remember you")
Simple Man by Lynryd Skynyrd
Aenema by Tool
Change (in the house of flies) by Deftones
Tearing Away by Drowning Pool
Right Now by Korn
Dressed in Black by Sia
Get Up by Korn
Narcissitic Cannibal by Korn
Young and Beautiful by Lana Del Rey
Pretty When You Cry by Lana Del Rey
No Easy Way Out by Robert Topper
Never Enough by FFDP
Dark Paradise by Lana Del Rey
Empty Gold by Halsey
Wrong Side of Heaven by FFDP
Our Destiny Lies Above Us by Hans Zimmer

TIMELINE

June 20, 2016

Our baby has passed away but my wife still has to deliver our unborn child.
She's born at 5:46 p.m.
Our baby is baptized by holy water from Pope Francis.
She's taken away 10:45 p.m.
We spend the night. Without her.

June 21, 2016

(Mom) wife discharged from hospital. We go home.
(Mom) wife has medical episode.
Meet with funeral director 2:00 p.m.

June 22, 2016

9:30 a.m., meet with Queen of Heaven Cemetery director
11:00 a.m., we bring Ashlyn's outfit to the funeral home. (Mom) wife sees her (you). She almost passes out. She has to be walked outside by the funeral director and me.
Emptiness.

June 23, 2016

9:00 a.m., viewing
10:00 a.m., funeral service
10:30 a.m., drive to the cemetery
10:45 a.m., we carried the casket to her grave. One person could carry the casket, but the four of us each carry one corner, my dad, my wife's dad, my brother, and myself. Prayers and words spoke at Ashlyn's grave.
11:30–2:00 p.m., luncheon at my parents'

June 24, 2016

Paid bills
Mowed grass
Played with Ryan outside
Cooked hot dogs
Olive garden dinner sent to the house by Ralph and Elyse
Mom and Dad come down to visit

In loving memory of my dear Ashlyn, though we only had a short time on this spinning blue marble together, you've taught me more than anyone ever could.

I love you so, so much.

Till we meet again.

Love Forever and Always,
Your Daddy

EPILOGUE

Healing can be found through remembrance. Remembering the child that you have and will meet again. I don't know what it's like to be a stillbirth mother. I could *never* say I know what it's like because I don't nor will I ever understand the pain of nurturing and carrying a child only to know one day the child is gone. I do know what it's like to be a stillbirth father. To feel useless and helpless to save the ones you love the most. I know what that feels like. Healing can only begin through remembering your child and forgiving yourself. Let go and place yourself in God's hands. Through faith and love anything is possible, no mountain too steep to climb and no journey too far to travel.

ABOUT THE AUTHOR

Andrew Yackuboskey is the author of *Ashlyn's Journal*, a true story account of the year following his daughter's death. He is a brother, a husband, and a father. He has four children—two sons, a daughter, and a daughter in heaven. He enjoys film, writing, fishing, and spending time with his family. He lives in Pennsylvania.